Santa Fe Trail
National Historic Trail

ON THE WESTERN PLAINS of the Oklahoma Panhandle, sandstone bluffs jut from the prairie to overlook Cold Springs Creek as it snakes toward its juncture with the Cimarron River. Countless traders, soldiers, gold-seekers, and others following the Cimarron Route of the Santa Fe Trail often camped by these bluffs and delayed their journeys long enough to carve their names in the soft stone.

At this place, appropriately called Autograph Rock, near Boise City, Oklahoma, the historic pageant of the Santa Fe Trail is recorded. Among the hundreds of names carved here are those of Hispanic traders and freighters, including Felipe Delgado, a Santa Fe merchant who carefully inscribed his name on the bluffs on at least three occasions. Not far from Delgado's "signatures" is that of Edwin Harrison, the 24-year-old son of a St. Louis entrepreneur who traveled the trail in 1860, and S. Brown, who passed by with Company F, Third United States Infantry, in 1859. Autograph Rock also bears carvings made by Indians living in the area years before Anglos and Hispanics knew of its existence.

Nowhere else is the true significance of the Santa Fe Trail so strikingly revealed. Here along Cold Springs Creek the inscriptions testify to a trail, a heavily traveled highway really, that bridged cultures, places, and changing times.

TRADE TO SANTA FE

The story of the Santa Fe Trail is closely tied to that of the commerce between Missouri and the Mexican frontier province of New Mexico. In 1821, William Becknell and five companions from Missouri's Boonslick

OPPOSITE: Wagon wheel ruts mark the Santa Fe Trail along Seneca Creek in northwestern New Mexico. Round Mound, a landmark in trail times, rises in the distance.

country headed west onto the plains, supposedly to trade with Indians for horses and mules and to catch "Wild Animals." But Becknell's intentions are questioned by some historians.

Nearly 900 miles to the southwest, in what was then a Spanish province, was a waiting market for textiles and other manufactured goods that traders—French, American, and others—had known about for years. Spain's colonial policy prohibited New Mexicans from manufacturing goods and trading with foreigners. But a few traders had ventured to New Mexico anyway and were able to both make a profit and escape the consequences of the law. Others, especially Americans, were not so lucky and quickly found themselves in prison and their goods confiscated.

Despite this well-known trade barrier, Becknell's party ventured deep into Spanish territory. Near the village of San Miguel del Vado, about 40 miles from Santa Fe, the party encountered a detachment of soldiers who, instead of placing the trespassers in irons, warmly greeted them. Becknell and his companions eagerly pushed on to Santa Fe, where his party was "received with apparent pleasure and joy." There he quickly sold out his small stock at a considerable profit and started back for Missouri, arriving in Franklin early in 1822.

The reason for Becknell's surprising success was that Mexico had achieved its independence from Spain only months before he arrived, and the old trade restrictions had been lifted. Becknell may have anticipated this revolution before departing and deliberately plotted a course for Santa Fe. Still, he and his companions had taken a serious risk that paid off better than anyone could have expected. Two other parties of Americans also journeyed to New Mexico in 1821, reaching the province before the dust kicked up by Becknell had settled. It was Becknell's achievement, however, that captured the imaginations of folks back in Missouri.

As a contemporary wrote in 1825, Becknell's "successful (for so it may be termed) expedition instantly excited many others to adventure to S[an]ta Fee." Indeed it did. At least three groups, Becknell's among them, left Missouri for Santa Fe in 1822. Foreseeing the enormous potential of the Santa Fe trade, Becknell transported his merchandise in three wagons, the first ever to be taken over the plains to New Mexico. These first few would be followed by thousands more in the decades to come, carrying large assortments of goods for the markets of the far Southwest and traveling what would become known as the Santa Fe Trail.

The most popular article in the Santa Fe trade was cotton cloth: printed (calico), bleached, and brown. Woolen and silk goods were also in demand in New Mexico, as was a remarkable assortment of odd items, from American playing cards to parasols. In return, the traders received silver pesos, mules, and asses, and early on in the trade, beaver pelts. In 1825, the value of goods taken over the trail to Mexico was estimated at $65,000. Ten years later it was $140,000, and in 1846 it was $1 million.

The Santa Fe trade was a major industry in the West, pumping vast amounts of silver coin and bullion into currency-starved Missouri banks. Numerous towns along the Missouri River vied to be the principal jumping-off point for Santa Fe, as such status guaranteed a thriving business in the outfitting of expeditions with supplies; the repair and manufacture of wagons, ox yokes, and harness; and the lodging of trail travelers. The trade was deemed so important that the United States government funded a survey of the route in 1825. A few years later, in answer to pleas from the traders, the United States Army began providing escorts to protect the merchant caravans from Indian attack.

Although called the Santa Fe trade, this overland commerce stretched far beyond the borders of Missouri and New Mexico, forming a link in the world trade of the time. Various European textiles were imported to the United States specifically for the Mexican markets. Santa Fe was only one of several destinations for the traders' merchandise. Many merchants traveled much farther south with their wares, to the towns of Chihuahua, Durango, Zacatecas, and San Juan de los Lagos. In 1846, trader Manuel Alvarez told a United States Army officer in Santa Fe that "most of the wagons go on to Chihuahua without breaking their loads."

The Santa Fe Trail was truly an international highway. By the 1840s, caravans belonging to Mexican merchants such as Antonio Jose Chavez, Ambrosio Armijo, Mariano Yrisarri, and Antonio José Otero were as

TOP: Independence, Missouri held sway as the trail's eastern terminus through the 1850s.

ABOVE: At Autograph Rock in Oklahoma, trail travelers inscribed their names at this popular spring and camp.

OPPOSITE: Outfitters such as Chick, Browne & Co. were the main suppliers of trade goods such as fabric, glass, and metal cookware. Bill of sale (above) and envelope (below) from Chick, Browne & Co.

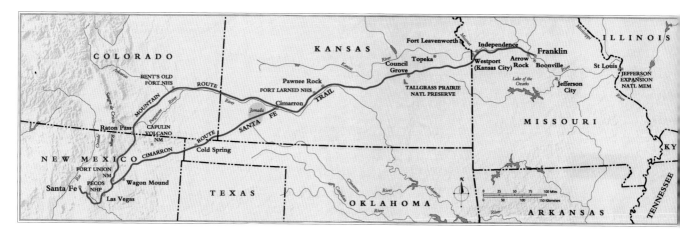

ABOVE: Through treaties, travelers along the trail gained permission to journey through long-established Indian territories.

common on the trail as those of James Magoffin, Henry Connelly, Charles Bent, and Samuel Owens. Despite various changes in the trade, including the effects of the Mexican-American War of 1846–48, Hispanic merchants retained an important role in this commerce to the last days of the trail, some even into the era of the advancing railroad.

THE ROUTE

The Santa Fe traders were not the first to traverse the region of the trail. Indians, Spanish explorers, and French traders had heavily trod the area long before them. But the annual merchant caravans quickly established a specific route across the plains that became as familiar as a St. Louis street, one that cartographers would locate on early maps as "Waggon Rd to Santa Fe," "Caravan route to Santa Fe," and "Santa Fe Trail."

The distance from Franklin, Missouri, the first trailhead, to Santa Fe was 865 miles. After the Missouri River flooded in 1828, much of the outfitting trade shifted farther upstream to the town of Lexington. The city of Independence, platted in 1827 in Jackson County, Missouri, soon succeeded Lexington and held sway into the 1850s. In fact, Independence was a popular rendezvous point for both Santa Fe traders and emigrants to Oregon. Other contenders for the eastern terminus of the trail were Westport, Missouri (now part of Kansas City), and Leavenworth City, Kansas. But beyond these particular communities, at least up until the time of the Civil War, the traders were guided on their journeys only by rivers, springs, natural landmarks, and the worn paths and eroded scars left by the wagons of previous seasons.

About 150 miles along the trail from Independence on the Neosho River was Council Grove, named for a treaty made there with the Osage Indians by the officials surveying the trail in 1825. At this scenic spot, later the site of a booming trail town, the traders organized their individual parties into a single command structure for mutual protection on the rest of their journey. Teamsters busied themselves chopping and hewing spare axletrees from the oak and hickory timber along the river, as these would be the last significant hardwood trees encountered on the route.

After leaving Council Grove the trail continued west/southwest until striking the Arkansas River at present-day Ellinwood, Kansas. From this point, the caravans roughly paralleled the left bank of the Arkansas, passing the well-known landmark of Pawnee Rock and eventually reaching the area of modern Dodge City. Most traders then forded the river at one of three primary crossings: the Lower Crossing (near Ford, Kansas), the Middle Crossing (actually varying sites between Dodge City and Charleston to the west), and the Upper Crossing (near Lakin).

The crossings marked the beginning of the Cimarron Route of the trail, the major obstacle of which was the *jornada*, a virtually waterless stretch of 50 to 60 miles (depending on which crossing was used) between the Arkansas and Cimarron rivers. Beyond the jornada, the Cimarron Route continued southwest, past natural landmarks such as Round Mound and Point of Rocks, until it united with the Mountain Route of the trail at present-day Watrous, New Mexico. The trail then wound through the towns of Las Vegas (after 1835) and San Miguel, passed the ruins of Pecos Pueblo, and surmounted Glorieta Pass to finally descend to Santa Fe.

The Mountain Route was another option for trade caravans venturing to the New Mexico capital. Instead of fording the Arkansas River at the crossings, they could follow the river westward, traveling what was sometimes called the "Bent's Fort Route," and later known as the Mountain Route. Just northeast of what is now La Junta, Colorado, the Mountain Route reached the famous adobe fort established in the early 1830s by William and Charles Bent and Ceran St. Vrain to trade with various Indian tribes. A few miles upstream from Bent's Fort, the Mountain Route crossed the Arkansas River and struck due southwest until it reached the base of the Raton Mountains (the trail town of Trinidad would be established here alongside the Purgatoire River in 1861). The mountains were

BELOW: Geologic features such as Round Mound were important navigational guides.

By the 1860s, the majority of wagons used on the trail were manufactured in the West.

crossed via the dreaded Raton Pass and the trail then continued southward, through the New Mexican settlements of Cimarron (after 1844) and Rayado (after 1848), until reaching its juncture with the Cimarron Route near Fort Union.

William Becknell had probably traveled much of what would become the Mountain Route of the trail on his first expedition to Santa Fe in 1821. It was because of difficulties his party encountered in crossing the Raton Mountains, however, that he took a different route with his three wagons in 1822, blazing portions of the Cimarron Route for future traders. Although occasional wagon trains braved Raton Pass in the late 1830s and 1840s, and again during the Civil War, the shorter Cimarron Route was the road of choice until it was bypassed by the railroads in the late 1860s.

SHIPS OF THE PRAIRIE

Merchant caravans could number anywhere from ten wagons to more than one hundred, making about 15 miles a day on the trail. Through the 1840s, most of the traders' wagons were of the famous Conestoga design, many of them manufactured in Pittsburgh. Trail traveler Thomas J. Farnham described them in 1841 as "long sunken Pennsylvania wagons" and stated that they were purchased in Independence during the outfitting season. But Pittsburgh manufacturers eventually faced stiff competition from Missouri wagon makers, men like Joseph Murphy and Louis Espenscheid of St. Louis, Hiram Young of Independence, and M. T. Graham of Westport. By the 1860s, the majority of wagons used on the trail were manufactured in the West.

From the 1850s on, the average load carried by these wagons was around 6,000 pounds. The draft animals used to pull the immense loads were either mules or oxen. Teamsters continuously debated the advantages of each. Mules were faster and could take heat and lack of water better than oxen. But mules were also more expensive, and they were the special target of raiding Indians. A herd of docile oxen was harder to run off and, in a pinch, the oxen would make a more palatable meal.

Colonel James F. Meline described the ox trains he saw in Leavenworth, Kansas, in 1866 as "remarkable, each wagon team consisting of ten yokes of fine oxen, selected and arranged not only for drawing but for pictorial effect, in sets of twenty, either all black, all white, all spotted, or otherwise marked uniformly." Whether pulled by mules or oxen, a long train of Santa Fe wagons with their canvas tops billowing in the wind was one of the great sights of trail days.

LIFE ON THE TRAIL

Although the trail thrived on commerce, all types of people used it, and for a variety of reasons. Many caravans included young men simply seeking adventure. The trail also attracted the afflicted who believed that the "purity" of the plains would cure them, or at least result in an improvement. Josiah Gregg, an invalid when he embarked with a wagon train on the Santa Fe Trail in 1831, was riding horseback and consuming large amounts of buffalo meat after just two weeks of life in the open. Following that initial trip, Gregg entered the trade himself and later wrote what is still the classic account of the Santa Fe Trail and trade, *Commerce of the Prairies.*

After gold was discovered in California in 1848, some groups of Forty-Niners traveled over the Santa Fe Trail for a part of their overland journey. Goldseekers again took to the trail after the discoveries in Colorado in 1858. The trail also saw countless soldiers, contract freighters, and a good number of emigrants in its six decades of use. Regardless of whom they were, all travelers faced the same hazards of trail life.

Weather on the plains often ran to extremes, from heavy rains that swelled streams to dry heat that shrank wagon wheels from their iron tires, causing wagoners to remove the wheels and soak them in streams and water holes. Violent thunderstorms erupted over the prairie in the spring, and upon their approach traders chained their wagons together to prevent their valuable cargoes from being upset.

Severe weather could be fatal for caravans that started for Santa Fe too late in the season. This happened to the trains of Albert Speyer and partners Henry Connelly and Edward James Glasgow. In October 1844 their Santa Fe–bound caravans were caught by an early winter snowstorm in the Oklahoma Panhandle. The storm killed about fifty of Connelly and Glasgow's mules; Speyer lost eighty. Their wagons were stranded on the trail until they could send to Santa Fe for more draft stock.

For those who desired a faster way to Santa Fe than that provided by the slow-moving ox and mule trains, stage service was available beginning in 1850. One-way tickets in 1857 sold for $125 (May to November) and $150 (winter). It was not exactly a first-class ride. Instead of the famous Concord coach, passengers often rode in light wagons called ambulances. Because stage stations were nonexistent between Council Grove and Fort Union, stages stopped for the night under the stars, some passengers

TOP: A thunderstorm hangs above Comanche National Grasslands in Colorado.

ABOVE: River crossings were the most perilous part of the journey. The best crossings contained bedrock, a more sure footing for teams of livestock.

OPPOSITE TOP: Covered wagons, pulled by teams of oxen or mules, held an average load of 6,000 pounds.

OPPOSITE BELOW: Bent's Old Fort National Historic Site was a prominent trading and mercantile stop along the trail during the first half of the 1800s.

curling up to sleep on the sacks carrying corn for the stage mules. Daily meals were cooked and served on the prairie. A stage traveler in 1853 described the passengers' camp table as an "india-rubber mule cover . . . spread upon the ground near the fire."

The accommodations for stage travelers improved somewhat over the years, but the ride itself still left something to be desired. An 18-year-old Ernst Kohlberg made the trip between Las Animas, Colorado, and Santa Fe in 1875 and wrote to his family in Germany that "traveling by stage is very tiring and strenuous. One cannot stretch out to sleep and if one could the continual bumping and jarring on the rotten roads would not permit any sleep, be it either by day or by night. Several times I was hurled from my seat and bumped the ceiling of the coach when we hit a bump real hard or went through an arroyo. It did not seem to bother the stage-driver if he upset the coach which happened several times."

The Santa Fe Trail passed through the territories and ranges of many Indian tribes, including the Pawnee, Arapaho, Cheyenne, Comanche, and Kiowa. The opening of the trail brought little that was beneficial to these native peoples, except perhaps for certain trade items and, more important, opportunities to steal the horses and mules that accompanied the caravans. The trail saw several periods when relations with the Indians were turbulent. Outrages committed by both sides resulted in conflicts that at times paralyzed trail traffic, particularly during the 1860s.

Yet for many travelers, encounters with Indians were important parts of the trail experience. Trader Edward James Glasgow wrote of his trading trips in the 1840s that the "moderate danger from Indians, kept up an excitement, not particularly unpleasant except for the trouble and constant watchfulness at night, to guard against stampedes." And those who experienced peaceful encounters often expressed admiration for the Indians they met. Artist and writer Heinrich Mollhausen met members of the Cheyenne, Arapaho, and Kiowa tribes along the trail in 1858 and wrote that "They were tall, well-built people, genuine inhabitants of the plains in whose posture you could not miss seeing a certain boldness, and in whose armour, Indian wealth. . . . The dress was different in the case of each native, and so gaily colored, so peculiarly adorned and cut that one involuntarily wondered at the gift of imagination of these people who knew how to express their taste in such varying and different forms."

One savvy trail traveler cautioned that "an Indian knows when he is abused and insulted, as well as a white man—and is as ready to resent it, and properly, too." William H. Ryus, a young stagecoach driver on the trail in the 1860s, found that when the Indians he encountered on his route were treated with respect and honesty, the courtesy was returned. Ryus often shared his coach's coffee, bread, and other provisions with passing

Preserving the Past

Congress designates national historic trails to commemorate and preserve the routes of travel that played a significant role in U.S. history. Trails follow the paths of traders and explorers, migrants, American Indians, military groups, and others. They are established to help identify and preserve historic sites and trail segments. Official trail logos, like the one above, lead the way for present-day travelers to retrace parts of the original routes.

The Santa Fe National Historic Trail is more than 1,000 miles long and passes through five states. Segments of the trail are owned and managed by private individuals, organizations, and public agencies. The National Park Service administers the trail through many partnerships to ensure visitors have places to experience the trail and learn about its history, thus preserving trail resources and stories for future generations.

Indians. He wrote years later that "if there were a large number of Indians, and our provisions were scarce, I would tell them so, but also tell them that notwithstanding that fact I still had some for them." Ryus proudly proclaimed that "at no time was my coach surrounded with hostile intent without departing from it in friendliness. At the same time I knew they had some great grievances."

There were other plains inhabitants that were sources of excitement and curiosity for trail travelers. These were the buffalo, elk, antelope, prairie dogs, and other wildlife. Buffalo received the greatest attention. Josiah Gregg notes that, on his first overland trip in 1831, some of the teamsters actually abandoned their wagons to chase the beasts on foot! While the buffalo generally lost in these encounters, the excitement that consumed their pursuers resulted in some minor victories for the hunted. An example was the outcome of a hunt by a party of Forty-Niners as recorded by Charles Pancoast: "One man, in attempting to take his Rifle from the pommel, discharged it, the ball entering his shoulder; another put a ball through the neck of his Horse; a third was thrown, and his Horse ran away with all his equipment and was never recovered."

Life on the trail, however, was not all prairie storms, Indians, and thundering herds. Many trips down the trail could be relatively uneventful, filled with long days followed by calm evenings around buffalo chip fires.

There were other plains inhabitants that were sources of excitement and curiosity for trail travelers.

Abundant game along the trail was a welcome source of fresh meat. CLOCKWISE: Mule deer, pronghorn, prairie dogs, lesser prairie chicken, and bison. OPPOSITE TOP: Markers designate segments of the trail.

ROAD OF WAR

The Santa Fe Trail was used twice for conquering armies. The first instance occurred during the war between the United States and Mexico. After the declaration of war on May 13, 1846, Colonel (later General) Stephen Watts Kearny was placed at the head of a 1,657-man invading force called the Army of the West and given two objectives: take and hold New Mexico and Upper California, and protect the American traders on the trail. The Army of the West departed Fort Leavenworth, Kansas, in units of varying size during June and July. Kearny's forces rendezvoused at Bent's Fort and from there continued down the Mountain Route of the trail, traversing Raton Pass on August 6 and 7. At their rear was a merchant caravan of approximately 150 wagons.

At Apache Canyon, through which the trail passed 15 miles from Santa Fe, New Mexican governor Manuel Armijo had assembled a large force of regular soldiers and militia to challenge Kearny. However, before the fast-moving Army of the West could reach this place, Armijo surprisingly disbanded his force and fled south to Chihuahua with a small body of his troops. The Army of the West marched into Santa Fe unopposed on August 18, 1846, and, in the words of Lieutenant W.H. Emory, "as the sun was setting, the United States flag was hoisted over the palace [of the Governors], and a salute of thirteen guns fired from the artillery planted on the eminence overlooking the town." Despite subsequent armed resistance, American control of New Mexico prevailed.

The Santa Fe Trail became the lifeline between the new territory and "the states," and it was deemed vital to protect the traffic and communications along it (regular mail service between Independence and Santa Fe began in 1850). Military posts were established along the trail to protect trail travelers and local citizenry from hostile encounters with Indians. These included Fort Union, Fort Wise (later changed to Fort Lyon), Fort Dodge, Fort Larned, and others. The increased military presence in New Mexico and along the trail also created a burgeoning demand for supplies, which resulted in major freighting operations and more business for merchants.

TOP: A sales receipt from merchants Otero & Sellar.

RIGHT: Otero & Sellar operated several locations like this one in Hays City, Kansas, that profited from the trade and travel along the trail.

OPPOSITE TOP: The army established Fort Union in New Mexico in 1851 to protect travelers along the trail. The site is now a national monument.

OPPOSITE BOTTOM: Fort commissaries, like this one at Fort Larned National Historic Site in Kansas, provided supplies to both military personnel and civilians.

In February and March 1862 a Confederate force from Texas, commanded by Brigadier General Henry H. Sibley, advanced up the Rio Grande Valley into the heart of New Mexico, occupying Santa Fe on March 10. The Texans' immediate goals were to seize the Territory for the Confederacy and take possession of the military stores there. Ultimately, Sibley hoped to capture the rich Colorado gold fields to the north. With the New Mexico capital now in Rebel hands, the next objective was to take Fort Union, 100 miles up the trail.

On March 26, in the same Apache Canyon traversed by General Kearny's columns sixteen years before, an advance detachment of the Texan army was surprised by more than 400 Union troops under the command of Major John M. Chivington of Colorado Territory. This contingent was part of a larger force made up of Colorado and New Mexico Volunteers and United States Army Regulars that had left Fort Union four days before. The Colorado troops, comprising approximately 75 percent of the total Union strength, had made incredible forced marches to reach Fort Union in time to defy Sibley's invasion. After a three-hour fight known as the Battle of Apache Canyon, thirty-two Confederates and five Federals were dead. The Texans retreated, leaving Chivington in possession of the field.

Two days later, the Texans again advanced with reinforcements up Apache Canyon and toward Glorieta Pass. In command of the roughly 1,100 men was Colonel William Scurry. Scurry's troops crossed Glorieta Pass and attacked the main Union force under Colonel John P. Slough at the ranch of Alexander Valle, known as Pigeon's Ranch. The Battle of Pigeon's Ranch, also called the Battle of Glorieta Pass, lasted six hours with Slough's force of about 900 grudgingly giving up ground.

Slough ultimately ordered a retreat, and it appeared that the Confederates had won a major victory. But as Slough and Scurry were battling at Pigeon's Ranch, a Union detachment under Major Chivington and United States Army captains William Lewis and Asa Carey had flanked the Rebel forces and discovered the lightly guarded supply train to the rear of Scurry's force.

Military posts were established along the trail to protect trail travelers and local citizenry from hostile encounters with Indians.

TOP: The Battle of Glorieta Pass was a turning point of the Civil War in the West. At the end of the three-day battle, the Union firmly controlled New Mexico and the Santa Fe Trail.

BELOW: The Santa Fe plaza bustled with trade, with goods coming in from the East as well as going out.

OPPOSITE: Wagon travel along the Santa Fe Trail ended with the arrival of the railroad in Santa Fe in 1880.

After a brief skirmish, the entire train was burned to the ground. With the destruction of these supplies the Texans abandoned all hope of reaching Fort Union, or even maintaining their foothold in New Mexico. The Confederates began their long march from Santa Fe back to Texas on April 7, leaving New Mexico and the Santa Fe Trail firmly under Union control.

THE RAILROAD

The extension of rail lines across the plains began in earnest after the Civil War. As steel rails crept closer to Santa Fe, so did the eastern terminus of the Santa Fe Trail. In 1867 it was Hays City, Kansas, on the Union Pacific Eastern Division (later changed to the Kansas Pacific). Three years later, the Kansas Pacific had crossed the western border of Kansas into Colorado Territory, establishing the new terminal town of Kit Carson. The entry of the railroad into Colorado marked the beginning of the Mountain Route's heyday. The Mountain Route was now more direct than the Cimarron, and a toll road had been opened over Raton Pass in 1865 with improvements such as bridges and cuts that made the ascent of the pass more negotiable for heavy freight wagons. The proprietor of this road was the old mountain man and scout, "Uncle Dick" Wootton.

In 1873, the Atchison, Topeka & Santa Fe Railway competed with the Kansas Pacific for the trail's business when its line reached Granada, on the Arkansas River in eastern Colorado. That same year, a branch line of the Kansas Pacific was built south, establishing the new railhead of West Las Animas (present-day Las Animas, Colorado) approximately 50 miles west of Granada. Both lines reached the site of La Junta in 1875, but the new town that sprang up there was left high and dry the next year by the Denver & Rio Grande, which ran a line south from Pueblo to within a few miles of Trinidad and Raton Pass, creating the railhead of El Moro.

Although these railroads moved rapidly across southern Colorado, eating up huge chunks of the trail at a time, the remaining portions of the old route to Santa Fe continued to see heavy use. Traffic and trade over the trail was still booming in 1878, as the *Colorado Democrat* reported on July 11, "Upwards of 500 freight wagons can be seen any day in El Moro. Probably 200 arrive and depart daily. These wagons come loaded with wool, hides and copper, and depart with merchandise and machinery for New Mexico and the Far South. The railroad has not the facilities for doing the business that is required."

Like the other railheads, El Moro's glory days as the eastern terminus of the Santa Fe Trail were brief. The Atchison, Topeka & Santa Fe built a line from La Junta to Trinidad in 1878, having beaten out the Denver & Rio Grande for the right-of-way

to Raton Pass. The Atchison, Topeka & Santa Fe now had what was left of the trail all to itself. In 1879 its rails reached the town of Las Vegas and in 1880 a spur was built from the main line at Lamy into the old capital. The first train arrived in Santa Fe on February 9. The days of lumbering freight wagons to and from Santa Fe were over, and the trail became a memory.

LEGACY OF THE TRAIL

Throughout its history, the Santa Fe Trail was a thoroughfare for change, whether desired or not. The trail, along with other forces of American westward expansion, helped to spell the end of a way of life for the Plains Indians. It also brought substantial change to the Indian (Pueblo and Navajo) and Hispanic populations of New Mexico, especially after the American occupation of 1846. But the Santa Fe Trail also opened the door for a rich exchange of ideas, languages, material culture, food, and more. This is probably the most important, and enduring, legacy of the trail. This cultural exchange continues in the American Southwest today.

In 1987, in recognition of its national significance, the United States Congress designated the Santa Fe Trail a National Historic Trail. This was the latest in a series of efforts to preserve and recognize the old route, which began with the marking of the trail by the Daughters of the American Revolution in the early twentieth century. Much of the trail remained when the Daughters set out to locate it, and so it does today.

Modern-day travelers can still see many of the famous landmarks of the trail, places with evocative names such as Rabbit Ears, Wagon Mound, and Starvation Peak. Traces of the ruts left by the traders' wagons can be found all the way from the Missouri River to Santa Fe, with long stretches visible in Kansas, Colorado, Oklahoma, and New Mexico. Stagecoach stops, forts, and homes of early-day settlers overlook the trail as they did more than a century ago.

The trail is also revealed in the many diaries, letters, and books left by historic travelers such as Lewis Garrard, Josiah Gregg, Miguel Otero, Marian Russell, and Susan Magoffin. The railroad may have ended their travels over the old trail, but those who choose to begin anew will find the Santa Fe Trail still offers an experience filled with discovery.

Other National Parks to Visit

Bent's Old Fort National Historic Site
Fort Larned National Historic Site
Fort Union National Monument
Pecos National Historical Park

Further Reading

Dary, David. **The Santa Fe Trail: Its History, Legends, and Lore.** New York: Penguin Group, 2002.

Gardner, Mark L. **Wagons for the Santa Fe Trade: Wheeled Vehicles and Their Makers, 1822–1880.** Albuquerque: University of New Mexico Press, 2000.

Gregg, Josiah. **Commerce of the Prairies.** 1844; reprint ed., Norman: University of Oklahoma Press, 1954.

Hyde, George. **Life of George Bent, Written from His Letters.** Norman: University of Oklahoma Press, 1968.

Otero, Miguel Antonio. **My Life on the Frontier, 1864–1882.** 1935; reprint ed., Albuquerque: University of New Mexico Press, 1987.

Russell, Marian Sloan. **Land of Enchantment.** 1954; reprint ed., Albuquerque: University of New Mexico Press, 1981.

Simmons, Marc, and Hal Jackson. **Following the Santa Fe Trail: A Guide for Modern Travelers.** Santa Fe: Ancient City Press, 2001.

Published by Western National Parks Association
The net proceeds from WNPA publications support educational
and research programs in the national parks.
Receive a free Western National Parks Association catalog,
featuring hundreds of publications. Email: info@wnpa.org or visit
www.wnpa.org

Written by Mark L. Gardner
Edited by Ron Foreman, Melissa Urreiztieta
Designed by M W Velgos Design
Photography by: front cover: Tom Bean, painting: Gerald Cassidy,
View of Santa Fe Plaza in the 1850s (End of the Trail), Collection
of the New Mexico Museum of Art, photograph by
Blair Clark; page 2: Adriel Heisey; page 4: Mark
Gardner; page 5: top: Courtesy Library of Congress,
LC-USZ62-3667, above: Tom Bean; page 6: Charles
Goslin, courtesy National Park Service; page 7: Andrea
Sharon, National Park Service; page 8: top: Ron Dulle; middle
and bottom: George H.H. Huey; page 9: top: Tom Bean; above:
Andrea Sharon, National Park Service; page 10: Tom Bean; page
11: Tom Bean (all); page 12: top: Courtesy of the New Mexico
State Records Center and Archives; right: Courtesy of the New
Mexico State Palace of the Governors; page 13: top: Tom Bean
(both); page 14: top: George H.H. Huey; bottom: Charles Goslin,
courtesy National Park Service; page 15: Denver Public Library;
page 16: Tom Bean.
Map by Eureka Cartography
Printed by C&C Offset
Printed in China

WESTERN
NATIONAL PARKS
ASSOCIATION

SANTA FE TRAIL
NATIONAL HISTORIC TRAIL